# Landscapes of Time

New, Uncollected, and Selected Poems

Alastair Macdonald

**BREAKWATER**

**BREAKWATER**
100 Water Street
P.O. Box 2188
St. John's, NF
A1C 6E6

*The Publisher gratefully acknowledges the financial support of the Canada Council, which has helped make this publication possible.*

*The Publisher acknowledges the financial support of the Cultural Affairs Division of the Department of Municipal and Provincial Affairs, Government of Newfoundland and Labrador, which has helped make this publication possible.*

*Cover photo: Dennis Minty*

*Author Photo: Margaret Miles-Cadman*

---

**Canadian Cataloguing in Publication Data**
Macdonald, Alastair.

Landscapes of time

(Newfoundland poetry series)

ISBN 1-55081-106-1

I. Title.   II. Series

| | | |
|---|---|---|
| PS8575.D6L36 1994 | C811'.54 | C94-950154-9 |
| PR9199.3.M33L36  1994 | | |

---

Copyright © 1994 Alastair Macdonald

Printed in Canada

# Acknowledgements

Some of these poems appeared earlier in *Aberdeen University Review* (U.K.), *Atlantic Advocate* (Canada), *Contemporary Verse II* (Canada), *English* (U.K.), *Fiddlehead* (Canada), *Newfoundland Quarterly* (Canada), *New York Times, Scottish Literary Journal* (U.K.), *TickleAce* (Canada), *Twentieth Century* (U.K.); in the anthologies *Banked Fires* (Canada), *Choice Poems of the Newfoundland Quarterly* (Canada), *East of Canada, First Prize-Winning Entries* in Newfoundland Government Arts and Letters Competition (Canada), *Live Poetry* (U.S.), *Modern Newfoundland Verse* (Canada), *New Voices in American Poetry* (U.S.), *Poets of Canada, Stroud Festival Poems* (U.K.), *31 Newfoundland Poets* (Canada); and in the author's previous collections *Between Something and Something* (U.K., 1970), *Shape Enduring Mind* (U.S., 1974), *A Different Lens* (Canada, 1981), and *Towards the Mystery* (Canada, 1985).

# Contents

## west wind

drive
         swift shadow of cloud, violet, silent
      contour-glide of plough and domed
tree-feathering this spring-or-autumn day,
      wind, straining tree-hair from hills' brow,
blowing dead leaves or is it husks of new
      in the pale red-green autumn spring
tugging: still buffeting with memory
      of what will come tomorrow
thirty years ago, and the long past
      tomorrow of today, the pain
of twenty, lingering of twenty's ache,
      and haze of beauty's proud illusion
for a time of permanence and meaning:
      in the dream-blend of my walking
over old ground these years back to the past
      on a day that's stayed through the ages
tossing one's thoughts into

                                    what now?

# TAMARA DESNI

When I was small grown-ups would smoke
and I had cigarette card albums,
all new worlds for me out there,
insects, locomotives, cars,
aeroplanes and cricket, ships,
the Bremen, Normandie, and Rex,
F. Woolley, G.O. Allen, Farnes, and look
at all the film-folk sitting in the air
of Hollywood:
                        George Arliss,
Richard Arlen, early Crawford,
Gable, Harlow, Carole Lombard and
Tamara Desni (just before
the climbing starburst shower of
Bett' or Betté Davis).
Baby Austins cost
a hundred pounds and
for a thousand you
could have that Rolls Royce
Phantom III.

I never (then or later)
saw Tamara Desni.
There was a butterfly too I
never saw — er ... Peacock, the
Something Peacock, or a ... It
had marvellous colourings with
roundels (air forces call them)
on the wings.

When it was Hitler's war
I, almost not a boy,
gave them with Meccano,
train sets, model planes (for when
might there have been more of these?)
to younger kids.

All rightly went,
though I've regretted them.

Our stars are different since,
but any time, as sparer now
the alms we give oblivion,
I see my childhood ones
on the TV (if not, even yet,
Tamara Desni).

Long
the butterflies had disappeared.
But they are back,
and today I found one
poised upon a hedge,
wings closed, the undersides
a glossy, velvet dark.
And when it started up
a glory flashed of yellow,
soft red, white, and peacock blue,
and the roundels on its wings.

## EARLY WAY

I drive the road
a child walked
who followed the lure.
Each turn remembered,
rise or view unchanged,
which know and share
my being then
but not the after,
pain that they hold
no pain.
Outward was long,
but I travel back
in minutes now
from where I've been.

# EQUINOX

Again at tide's race and the salt howl
of a year's turning, self's nurtured calm
shatters, thoughts fling as veering gull

feather and dried leaf on emotion's upswing
and down with gales sweeping day's cloud-rack
and loud in the night's hollow chimney sounding

emptying sense of purpose uncaught. And cracked
egg and bleached bone lie clean on shore,
function complete, with a finish we have lacked

in the still proceeding not-yet of our
part's ending. Presumption of wider meaning
than in submission to the surge as nature

courses gives only disturbance dragging
in powerful undertow: divided pull
of earth, and lift of a glimpsed whole eluding.

# MINISKIRT

Child,
grown to the fancied daring
of sixteen:
eyes blacked, corpse-lipped,
hair down, farouche:
the whore-look of time past
hallowed today
by fashion-house decree
into a guise
for innocents;

self-consciously possessed
in brazen black and sexy shine
of metal,
patent gloss, and leather;
or slim or vast in shifts,
exposing knobbled knee
or thigh tremendous;
Picasso parody
of human shape
and line:

grotesquerie:
the calculated awkwardness
nose-thumbing at proportion
and stale authority;
the new-old flout which says
look, look,
only such youth as this
of mine
can dare;

with twitchings,
kicks, kinks, quirks,
you pass
along the sidewalks,
brief in skirts,

tapering in tights,
eyes for the boys,
on teetering, tic-tac steps
on pinhead
heels;

or sit
in cafés, bars, and dives. —
Child eyes
look out
from hanging screen of hair
and haze of rebel cigarette;
playing the game of temptress;
wanting,
yet afraid to be what you would seem.
Innocence
through bold stare
says 'Is this right?
Is this the way of it?'
And laughter at the role
not quite believed in
breaking
the mask.

Seize, laugh;
enjoy
the smooth-skinned fun of it.
Not many years will pass
before
you cannot well afford
this luxury
of ugliness.

# ENDING

The poem was never ended, but the draft
survived, nearly complete, clear enough
to be worth finishing. So I tried;
succeeded up to a point. And yet

it wasn't right. Something didn't emerge
from words about love parted on the ragged
page of thirty years ago. Some essence
from when life vibrated with supposed

import, elusive then, gone utterly now.
And I, editor only, couldn't find
the statement which evaded a young poet;
and knew that we missed one another

over the common ground of the words
and a meaning half-caught, an experience
not to be shared: some truth twice lost,
first by my youth, now by the deadening years.

# WEDDING DAY

They are marrying someone in the church.
Old church in a country town.
Who knows how old —
grown part of the ground,
held together now with S's of iron.
And by the porch,
two photographers from the local paper
wait in the afternoon,
bored,
outside the closed doors.

Sun glints on black cars with the bride-ribbons.
Clouds break the blue.
Swans on the water
are white gliding question marks,
lovely, brutal, and crust-hungry,
in the moving, shadowed sunlight of a day
tricked out
with the painful beauty of summer.

At the alms house across the green,
old, beneath the verandah,
in the shade,
alone,
a woman sits,
watching the scene in the light;
remembering perhaps such an hour
or all from far time,
as she waits,
that had flowed down
to here.

At the church door sound claps up
with the movement of emergence.
People in black and white,
rose-, blue-, and magenta-hatted,

reverently high, relief-loud,
bunch
in the dazzle of sunshine:
advance triumphant, and blind
into the stretching years
that will make little difference
to this old church:
heirs to habit of lifetimes,
obedient
to the sad necessity of hope.


## NUITS DE MAI

Chestnut blooms finger
flying shredded cloud.
In lengthening nights
boys bike to country towns,
from corner cafés
shout at girls,
assault with laughter,
eyes.
Face hair
curls in tendrils
like the shooting vines.
Soon the scent of lime flower,
harvest of wine.
Now their motorcycles
roar spring ways.

# TRAFFIC

Crossing,
I see the dog's tongue
loll
as he pants while the car
waits at the lights.
The boy's arm is round his neck.

I am ten and my friend and my dog and my sister
are with me and dad and mum in front and we are
going as planned where we want
in the expectant warm throb of the car

I am ten and I am eight and I am forty
and I am three in humanly computed dog years
and I am here with my mum and dad and my brother
and his friend and my sister and children and
my wife and husband

and there are ten or seventy years or thirty more
to come.

And now
all is young young and strong
purposeful at the beginning
and permanent-seeming
in the midst of things
(while we think we have purpose)
as the car waits at the lights
to accelerate into
the forwards.

## THE HOLIDAY

She sat on a bench
of the promenade;
beside her stood the man —
a couple, elderly
though not yet old,
come from a northern land
into the sun
on holiday.

Behind her, sea —
all round
noon's shimmering play
on motion,
blue, green, white
on blue, and red,
of buildings, palms,
beach parasols;
on railed parade
flags flying,
people criss-crossing by,
and cars' demented congestion,
with din of hoots and shouting
in the heat.

About her a crowd
collecting — not a crowd,
a gathering, embarrassed, loose,
detached and yet concerned,
pausing and moving on.
One shook his head.

The ambulance had been called.
For she'd been stricken
in the sun
after just a day or two —
her skin still light.
And at this time
there was no more to do,

except for her
find strength
to wait.

And the traffic moved past them,
and the people, bare-limbed, brown,
in a coloured rag-bag of clothes,
the young and not so young and old,
but mostly young,
enacting in August heat
lustration in sun,
blue water,
making with single aim
the holiday they'd come for.

And she sat there waiting to be removed,
among people passing and looking,
willing the strength to sit upright,
to give reassurance, quieten alarm,
in outward refusal to bow to the need.

'You'll be all right ...', he said,
perhaps believing it.
But, till she looked away,
frozen with what she knew
her eyes held mine as if for help,
I, stranger, helpless at the edge,
and we both sensed we knew
there was no journey back
for her to home, familiar life,
this was the journey back,
the start and ending of
the holiday.

What had they come for?
He to give her rest and change.
And she? To accept the gift,
though anxious at first venturing so far;
yet more than this —
a secret wish
to live again a girl's sensations,

long years fled,
but caught sometimes in flashes,
oftener now:
the joy of sunlight youth was bathed in,
sun through leaves on summer mornings,
glints on flowers or water,
bringing a sense of something just to come
and make one glad.

And they had come
and known the sun on sea,
and sunlight blazing, burning
in the height of day —
she dry and burning
in her back and throat,
yet cold,
in a scene that swam
and blurred
at first fade-out.

But thought lived yet.
The eyes showed that.
They tried to say
what could not now be voiced.
His head was bent to catch.
For her today
something had come
out of the bright and sparkling light
resisting resistance,
not to be repelled;
the moment, imagined
sometimes in a life,
without, as must be,
means to imagine (what
will it be like?),
considered and dismissed
(the heart will not accept)
to future time:
the knowledge sensed
of something ended now
in flagrant noon of foreign day

whose end she would not see —
the twilight wash of amethyst
and velvet darkness — suddenly
a lifetime ended and no power
to do what must be done,
to say what should be said
and so much else
unsaid a lifetime cannot say:
all that had meaning ended in
a place of passage, beautiful
but meaningless.

About them people passed,
among the cafés, shops,
expending currency
on tourist bric-à-brac,
useless eye-catching trash,
and sometimes better things
and postcards prettier
than what they're of
in harmless coloured lie.

For her
light going out there
in the light.
And with no rage.
Only the quiet
of a courage,
fear.

And the ambulance screamed
at last into the midst
and scattered gazers with
hysteric hew-haw bray,
and she was gone,
he too
to be with her
for what remained,
on waves of hew-haw terror
in the glare.

# VIALS

Reading (sometimes) my own poems
I'm struck by how they'll let out
whiffs of the sentient flowering
that seeded them. This apart

from content perhaps no longer
believed: or if that's too strong —
each came about when it had to,
couldn't again from one's now.

So poems may be signatures
in sand, thread of feeling's drift,
thought, webbed in spun rhythm and sound.

But better than the diary,
like a scent or the Vinteuil phrase,
they unstop the self which was.

# VAUX-LE-VICOMTE

High-hatted, erect on seat of water,
she fronts you with dowager hauteur,
no more than a shade wan
from centuries' homage to her spell. And then
on south façade the gold smile of the bow,
radiant to far point of vista-ed geometry.
Inviolate still, who in her youth
saw the best of the Grand Siècle:
Lully, Molière — all that.

Today, a July morning, two or three
wander the sun-dried emptiness: girls jeaned,
a woodsman puttering distance on a bike.
Where the long transverse canal dies through
to mud pool in the trees, boys fish,
as forebears did from those razed villages.

                              But not to slight
a splendour as of too high cost.
Now, the creation lures, because apart,
in grandeur and planned peace,
asserting what, with luck, a mortal caught
in way of paradise.
Dream of a doomed Icarus, but made
by genius, and in time to stay,
a tribute to that taste.

Let them not pass to vandals, and the sheep
of Philip Larkin's churches: Blenheim,
Chatsworth, when His Grace no longer can.

Prised out of pigeon-holes and cares,
here we may yet touch space,
in scent of box and water breathe the years.

# POPULAR SONG

We go for a summer meal
foie gras, chilled consommé
young pigeons stuffed with
kernels of pine
salad, cheese, a cool sorbet
champagne and other wine
the petits fours
by hey-hey hey hey
the waiters exude
cigarette breath
plates food
         savour of
cigarette breath.


         Old hags
in the gladdest rags
with all the bags
of longest wealth
are like Great Auntie Clay
my momma often had to stay.
She likes to cuddle little ones
so treat her right —
my momma long ago would say —
and all she has'll be yours
some day.
Aunt trotted globe from year to year
upped, offed according to her mood
hob-nobbed with baronets and earls.
With golden hair in towering curls
she was fat and silky soft and smooth
lumpy with emeralds and pearls.
Scented by Roger et Gallet
Guerlain, Chanel, and Guy Laroche
Lanvin, Patou, and Givenchy
she felt, smelt, tasted
oh so good.
But I screamed and screamed

and beat her for
she had ...


                      Cigarette breath
is the worst turn-off.


The wedding's set
the invitations out
Mama's ecstatic
who am I to doubt?
His kiss was like
salt ocean dawns
the suction as
the sea anemone
his tongue ...
Now fearful of impending yoke
or for some other reason he's
begun to smoke
has
cigarette breath.


Cigarette breath
cigarette breath

if you smoke
you've got
cigarette breath


cigarette breath
cigarette breath

you can't not have
cigarette breath


cigarette breath
cigarette breath

cigarette breath
cigarette death.

# DOUBLE FEATURE

TV
releases films
from my life-ago boyhood.
The stars were old adults then.

Grown young,
they are now all
beautiful, smooth-faced people.

I try
to find myself
between us, but see only
their eyes that look and wonder

who are these agèd voyeurs.

# TV NEWS

Through the blind eye, groomed and deodorized,
expression in place for the cameras,
the newsreader nightly conjures
youth's protest against itself,
the violence of peace marches.

Confessional tones, remoter than insult,
impersonal concern virulent as sadism
(and he no doubt the best of men)
materialize the nude child ballooning with hunger
the war victim terrorized, mangled, and shot.

They do not quite pass into the room.
Our nerves reject them, flick, while the image flicks
as if it had not been, to sweeter things:
nature, evocative dreams, the race's
idealisms, and averted wrongs.

But they are glimpsed, and root unquiet seeds.
Coexistent misery shares our tended calm;
implants a need to live this horror too
or be apart, impaired in the look for what
holds incompatible scenes in meaningful view.

# LIKE THY GLORY, TITAN

Cold stars clang shivering overhead
and Libra balances. Dawn's grey.
And then the sun
bursts like a fist of fires.
A woman hangs out wash.
In a sudden gust the clothes
she wears
strain with the wind's strength
from her in solid flow, like those
of the winged Niké in the Louvre.
Things whip, fly off the line.
Day and night are now, it's said,
of equal length.

Prometheus long since
stole fire, and sorely paid
for this to help us prove
though low, of dubious worth
what we might be instead.

We've had the fire, how long is it —
the godly secrets to advance
our state. How, after all this time,
when gathered power to build and save
is, in our nature, equal force
to break, will the balance tip?
And will our scale drop to the dark
or hover at uncertain par,
at best a headless victory.

The nights are deepening now. Though far
ahead in nature's year, and safely out
of our control, there is the rise
to light.

      If it's so in the year too
of our race, may we the less dread
the ball of fire and sudden flight
of rags and flesh in stripping flow
on the dire self-cleansing gale we've made.

# IN PERPETUAM REI MEMORIAM

They still observe, at memorials no longer
quite sacred, the silence of remembrance;
rifle-volleys catapult birds, and the brass bands,
sharp-tipped velveting, tongue solemn music.

Once, I looked at our training-barracks — abandoned,
home for the unhoused; washing, babies, dogs
in the old ordered, inhuman, company lines:
and wondered why it seemed so desolate.

In memory I route-marched again that landscape
of youth, hedgerow clay and field, chalk upland,
fenced from open range to embrace a springing love,
and with longings cloud-sped above highway.

And have outlived that old terrain of must, which now
oddly treasured blends with other country,
childhood, maps of a future; have marched decades far
into the soldier's dream of his freedom:

escaped, then, the ultimate moment, whether met
log-frozen, in atoms, or as sleeper
in sun-frothed vale: one whose skies would hurry yet, lift
the swirling dust of April purposes.

We, granted stay, ununiformed still march to find
some offering for the waiting moment,
having done what we might and known the painful stretch
between the fancied and the possible.

And it's not much good asking if one has failed them
whom ceremony honours here, or failed
the life one was. We move in the successive nows;
contend with change beyond and in the self.

And whether the sacrifice is any longer
useful is not the point. It is the then
we reverence. Their now and ours are not the same,
and hard to tell what continuity.

Only, either needs wrestle, scrutiny; and if
our interests and acts outreach the plain
selfish, we may have title to be here: in this
day perhaps will somehow find our giving.


## AMBITION

All the time one hears of young men
moving place and on to better jobs
or different positions, which they take
to be improvements of their situation

as far as they can judge, and which often
are, no doubt. And one hears of older
men, and old men, doing the same:
becoming directors and presidents; even

at their age climbing who have already
climbed. Not of course with similar motives.
Not for instance to support love and marriage,
now achieved or abandoned presumably,

or never attempted. For by this time
some sort of working relationship
has been established with one's wife:
the children are up: they may care for one
or not, but, in any case, for the most
part they have their own lives:
and even the love you hope for,
and with luck are sometimes given, must
be shared. Or there has been none
of all this; and it seems no longer a matter
of great importance. Either way
time shows how much we are alone.

Alone by oneself; alone in marriage and family
with a different and sometimes more complete

kind of loneliness, for we had once thought
these would remove the responsibility
of self. But it tends to stay with one
like conscience or anxiety making demands,
requiring attention, and in the last account
we find we have always been driven
by some need to satisfy it, gratify,
propitiate this god-creature of assertion
with sacrifices of things done, made, produced,
in the vain hope that we may so buy

peace. Few have the strength just to be;
and we go on into age, doing as long
as we are able whatever we think we can,
or wish we hadn't begun, trying to do

it better, or turning to something quite
different, blaming economic necessity,
our wives, or almost anything but the demon
that urges us on to fulfilment and repute.

## WITNESS OF PASSAGE

In snow, scoring the whiteness,
threaded prints of a creature
chart where it's come from, gone to,

may tell what it is, or does
with no aim to leave trace —

for a night, or a freezing.

Marks that would live
must stamp down
through the drifts of our timefall.

## GREEN ACORN

Just in
from a walk, I finger
an acorn I was moved to pick:
a shiny bullet, hard,
colour of jade, tight
in the briar-rough
stemmed bowl.

It has had no doubt
its one-in-a-somethingth chance
to yield lifetimes
of home and buttressing
to other creatures for a wheel
of centuries, or hide
whatever may have to be hidden
in oak trees
some far off nowadays.

I don't think I've had one
in my hands
since when they were gathered
for a treasure cache,
or in brown dried ripeness,
ball released from cup,
with twig in mouth
could be pretend-smoked
as big men's pipes.

In a day or two
it will be thrown out,
with the refuse
or on one of the first
rekindled autumn hearths,
with not even
the mere span of those
sixty years.

## COUNTRY BUS

The bus passes at its contained pace
along roads heavy with the trees of July.
As it turns a corner, thrusts of branches whang
on the sides and roof, so that, behind glass,
one instinctively flinches; and the small boys
who occupy the front seats duck
and make piercing dive-bombing noises.

I sit next to a window on the top deck.
Outside are fields of wheat yellowing
between hedges dark green still:
a landscape separated from me, set back
as in frame, cloud-shadowed, changing
from moment to moment, but always composed;
in some proportion; calm and affirming.

Often there are living beings in it: added
colour and movement. From time to time the bus
stops. A woman with a basket has
to get off, or one of the landscape figures gathered
at the roadside enters, and becomes a human,
a factor, capable of audible noises,
having crossed from there to here. Then on again.

Out there, a world of glassed-off distance
lies flattened, diminished, silent; meaningful
with a meaning one cannot name. Dimensional,
without dimension's impingement on the sense.
One would like to be part of it as
it appears, serene real the mind has made,
through the top windows of the moving bus.

While the slow journey lasts, and we proceed
with soporific throbbing and jolting among
the copses and fields to the next town,
the active self is necessarily poised between
whatever has just been left behind,
and what we imagine we are going to;
and we may wish sometimes it would not end.

But at last, with our stop, we have to go below
and out into the picture that is picture no longer.
Proportion disintegrates with the insistence of near
over far. Coherence dissolves; and now
from the composition things rush and leap
at us with movement and noise: engulfing waves
of circumstance with which we have to cope.


## BYPASS

A last bulldozer, clawing, snarled its bites
of soil down slopes; blue-reeking tarmac
was hot-ironed on; the new straightened road
ramped up from the bent bridge in the valley
was finished in April.

Crude in the spring landscape,
inverted nail-paring of earth raw red,
skid for cars going this way and that way. —
Later they sowed the sides with grass seed.

And in September, astonishing, there
in tired fields, leaves rattling towards fall,
the grass grew as spring, emerald-vivid
and shining as grasses in April,

smelling of April, in autumn already
far distant, of startings and freshness
at time of check and suspension and ache
for the spring, as ageing I walked
in that strange coexistence.

## CROSSING ENGLISH COUNTRY BY TRAIN
## IN LATE JULY

The ochre wash of wheat
floods in light-sheened waves
to rise about jade trees,
rust farm buildings, cottages.

For an instant composed,
though next seconds dissolving,
reforming, the picture springs
a surge of astonished peace
beyond the word.

Someone may be looking,
feeling, from the houses
islanded in corn. Their fixed view
is the sea of ripened field
awaiting the combines.
The susurration of its dryness
whispers autumn,
the heady edge of cooler,
cutting air through heat, and nights
of moonlit, almost
melancholy promise.
A train is skylining
the level wheat horizon,
carrying people through,
beyond its bounds,
to what, it might be fancied,
enviable magic?

The autumn ushered stir
as, in a different way, the spring.
Summer fulfils its life
but not always the dreams
it flowers in us.
From flying cloud unreached

the fall's start returned
the manageable self.
In time, these states
were more recalled than felt.

Or from above, the leisured
helicoptered hovering look
on the tawny patchwork
veined with green, where the local
diesel commuter,
a shortish, jointed grub,
boring this way and that,
noses the banks and hedges.

In the train,
through successive assemblages
of landscape, they are moving
perhaps to a point of view
sought still.


## PATHETIC FALLACY


Shy of the voiced goodbye,
concerned June flowerings high
in grass stir sentiently.
Your lost home glimpsed once more,
this annual pilgrimage,
you now must go. We too,
not yet, but soon:
won't know, who've but this year,
if you return again.

## HANDEL MASON

The dove road turns
this winter journey, skied
with summer's blue and white
quadrilles.
I park my motorbike and find
the cemetery,
off the track a little,
out of sight.
Boxed
in grey walls, stones still assert
incised identities,
soldiers, prisoners interred
with decency and military honours,
the plot restored by troops
posted in recent troubles,
and the grass cut only yesterday.
Guidebook and histories tell
of convicts from the hulks bleeding
a naval base,
death from yellow fever, and I see
their spot on this isle of the far hook
where buildings decay,
metal rusts,
elegized by wind clean and empty,
rip
of periodic ferry,
water's flick to shore
from peacock tides.

Voyaged to this shipwreck,
later, routine sea venture,
come to these yellow sands
captives of law and service
and due deliverance made.
Robed justice done no doubt:
today who knows

what slammed them off from theirs
to penal labour in a gold and turquoise
drift of land and space.

Poor wanderer
for some pretence of summer
soared in anaesthesia's
throbbing ride of the islands'chain
breathing the spiralling sun.
Their stillness spits
in beauty's taunt.
Thomas Jeffries 1853
deeply regretted by his fellow prisoners
Handel Mason private 2nd Bn
the Worcestershires at Watford Island
23 'Thy will be done.'

Shift of wind
out of the blue promise
separation of the ship,
devils here of rain and lightning,
roaring war of waves.
Twenty-three is no great age,
time yet for dreams' chase
in the head,
hope from senses' surge
that all will go right
under the beckoning skies.
Honour of country, empire, formula
of solace;
independence, freedom's jackboot,
other names,
now sanction blood.

Fall, drown
under the whelming tide
of urge to dominate,
destroy.

Elsewhere still we bury men
before their hour who die
we say
for some arrangement,
buying settled course
or change,
for not to die is other death:
sanctify
the kill it seems
that we must
                    make.

One in earth as in misery
they are here
I am there always
crowded by me
sightseers shoppers bathers
in towns and on beaches
thousands
shuttered gaze on the forward
thrusting the drive
which can be solitary
to self's meeting of sky and land.
Come a long way
to civilization's high
we blink out
putrid glint
of today's corpse in ditch by the roadside
the mutilation
the hollow-eyed whirlpool of pain
blackly questioning
beyond protest and comprehension:
something saying we have bred these looks,
the laced and spasmed shapes
which are not ours.

A turn of the road
mocks pleasure's chase

with the discovery of a grave:
names expendable,
a phase's sacrifice
and no one put there now.
Ended,
a boy from Worcester, Gloucester,
or other birdsonged
blossomed shire
with a musical parent and a need
to go with what was possible;
left in the green night
of alien loveliness,
sadly, we say, as if the dead flesh felt.

Prisoned
in the strange necessity
of wrong
we
need a magic,
even rough,
to set us free,
journeying to lie somewhere,
round what corner.

# THE GREENHOUSE

Shattered by spring gales, never
robust, it framed three generations.

Warm in winter from pipes and systems,
in summer wide-vented for coolness,
roof-glasses on the move a lifetime
with cloud on blue,

sixty years, transparent, frail, it kept
calendars of seed and ripening,
held the forms of my people tending
happiness, at least serenity:

one of the rarer places housing
nothing sad or dark unless
at partings when my mother went
to touch a flower, manage feeling.
And even then a restoration.

Today it's gone, and perhaps because
(in the disclaiming, quieting phrase)
by act of God
one seems less harmed.

But with it, a focus for images
of those meaning most to me, so that
there's now a further reconstruction
for memory to make.

# FROM MILLINGTON ROAD, NEWNHAM

Blocking my look across the fields
to Grantchester, a college reared
(alas St. Catherine's, for it is
their land) a high, three-storeyed range
of graduate student housing
(they may well call it) not unlike,
if larger, workers' dwellings which
the railway companies ran up
between the Old Queen's jubilees
in Swindon, Crewe, or Basingstoke,
of rankling red in rows on rows,
though sometimes nudging artistries
with modes of varicoloured brick.
(O Keble quad. O Ruskin stone.)
It has imposed a different view.
The woman, English from her air,
unstudied gestures, facing one
now above the back garden's length
sits flipping over single leaves
of what she's written (typed, processed),
bunching, and squaring edges so
that from the doubleglazed-off, hushed,
and picture-framed bright flowering scene
in fancy can be heard the thwack
on desk of the evened, done-with-
for-now phase of some last days' work.
Forceful movements as she dumps down
a drinking-mug, tosses her hair,
short thick a Glenda Jackson bounce
and swirl, jumps up to disappear
back into the room on a flounce
of seeming petulance. Well, no.
I've that thought too. But over there
my panes are black glass in the light,
mirror trees, the moving cloud. She
flounces with impatience at her

lover (assume), not live-in here
I think (for sometimes she's away
for long weekends, to the B.L.
perhaps, or else ...), just life, her work's
progress, a deadline's closure, too
much coffee whatnot any hour,
or just the genes she started with.
Her flouncing's bothersome. She'd be
a handful, that one.

                              Summer past.

This (only then I'm here), she's gone.
She had not yet when I left last
summer (although not suddenly).
A youth shows in the same window,
arrived today. Up, down, advance
recede stoop reach, straighten full height,
unpacking, setting book and book
on shelves. He sits, then sharply springs
to cross the room and fetch. He stays
at the desk once more a second,
turns and darts off to fade from sight
then flops at the desk again. No
concentration I'd infer. An
Eastern, skin opaque and pale. Hair
smooth, dense, and uniformly black.
China, Japan, Hong Kong. These days.
A summer school, some transient course,
English, computer science, oh
it could be anything. But soon
begins a stretch of toil head down,
ten hours a day with just snatched food.
He must be either brilliant or ...
for who but such could keep the pace.
And true, after two weeks of this
he's off again some days, then back,
not at the desk but out and in.

Absent more time. Returns to pack,
and on a Monday leaves for good.

                    Who are they really,
in their lives? I could, I suppose,
research. But no, they just impinge,
a little while, upon one's view.
Sad in a way, but then …

                              So you
have time to notice? Well, my stream
is silted, slow, and meanly I
resent the unthought mute reproach
of their mimed flow of industry,
the page on page of something done,
their sense of being in control
of things and days. For I was there
then (not here) like them at the door
of academia. From now
I see my flight has not been far,
or high in that empyrean.
My verse, later assumed, no more
received, remarked, not unjust end
for what is unremarkable.

These new raw buildings do not close
the old prospect quite, and beyond,
between the walls where there is space
meadows stretch still, and in long
azure days, puff clouds inch by, race
to the summer's self-tuned song.

## VOCABULARY

its better now
for we
schoolage guys
you dont have to sweat
what was called
vocab
like in olden days

three words
like n stuff
check
four
n stuff like that
is all

n youcn vary —
n stuff like
n like stuff
n like like
n that stuff like
like n that stuff
n like stuff that

thisll do
for anything
you have to explain

n theyll last you
into adult life

## AS THE MINISTER ELUCIDATES TO OUR INTERVIEWER

… it was broken.

Now regrouped we take your offer to confront
oh or engage oblige this media. We
the Government can apprehend too well
anxiety igniting from the present
deluge of events hail of statistics
which …

> What? No. I can't in this contingency
> reduce to specifics or name names
> should you have been following you
> must gather what
> I just infer
> to

action has been even as we speak
taken to dramatically target out
the root cause of the problem maximize
the nation's vast …

> > *if* I might *just* be let
> > go on

we shall see proof
from the cost-effective user-friendly cuts
we shall have brought on board of the kind
of turnround recognized worldwide I
and my colleagues have been thirsting towards
the vast majority of my time
in office …

> Well, a month

having said
that my clarification will not seem

over the top if I add that we do
not have to take the heat …

> I've yet to *see*
> a kitchen

from the hardliners I
have never ever once
been quailed by them as neither
parliamentary secretary or
now as you remind so recently a
Minister …

> Night through a glass darkling thickens as
> you put it.
> Funnily enough yourright.
> What I am saying will
> not give our game away before
> it's up — er won. The Opposition?
> The Old Possum. Have you seen
> it slinking
> in the shrubbery lately? Ha!  Aha!

But that's what politics are all about.
There are much to on a current basis address.
Lawrnorder an of our time phenomena
its breakdown by who started who
can know ever a naughty
for we Cabinet.
Recession.  Strife.  The list
goes on and on.
But of us noone
ever hopefully
can say
too little
too late.
And furthermore
if I may add

or presage
if you will
if you like
if you will
like when this slump
by our tactics
unpinned have
bottomed out
the cutting edge
of our policy
will be seen to
basically be
unsheathed ...

What's that? A photo-opportunity?

## A PAINTED DAY

The towered June trees
fend off the silk sack
of the day's heat
in lowering press
from skies of sulphurous grey.
Some fire leaks down as yellow
into the groves' tank
of leaf and filtered light
near Byron's pool,
to stripe with alternating shade
the packed clay path between the trunks,
a Corot 'Entrance to the Wood.'

It's a day for being young, whole,
with the boys who fish
the water-floated cloud
above the weir,
patiently avid
as Constable's Waltonians
in 'Stratford Mill.'

Sound barely elbows through
the torpid air,
a farm tractor's whir,
the stifled thunder of a jet
in undulating claps.
The meadows open, flat
between the hedges sugared high
with bloom of elder and wild rose.
Through hazed sun's champagne dance,
in the reaching flowers, the long grass,
or under wool-ball willows
forms are spaced,
some adults, children, dogs, a punt,
as if touched in by the brush
of a Monet or Renoir
on those fields along the Seine,

shaping, as they sit or run,
most likely unaware,
memories for themselves.

A day of a kind
we once felt cry
for something to be done,
made, captured and held fast;
but which, if not, would no less be,
and would pass over us
just the same.
A day like those merged now
in the glow of far recall,
too spun of dreams,
we think, to have been real.

Yet such are, still,
it seems.

# ART

Outside the window,
wide to its balcony rail,
the sun shines
on the June
horse chestnut trees.

Like a figure in a painting,
a Bonnard perhaps,
a little girl
bounces a knee-high ball.
The sun electrifies her hair
with a charge of frizzed gold.
Oscuros are mauve.

She knows nothing
beyond the pleasure
from the green and orange
stripy bump,
and of that too
she quickly tires and moves
away.

Creators shape
such elements,
by gift,
the layered skills,
sometimes shadowing import,
not always with intent
to mean,
and it may seem
a brush with insight
has been caught:

make works
reviewers, critics, then
will explicate,

or often
re-invent.

# REMEMBERING MY GRANDMOTHER'S BIRTHDAY

Gusts and rain today.
All day I've lived the brightness
of the life you spent
for those you loved, and bring
the only offering, thanks
for its span of selfless giving,
now just bauble berries cling
to tree and hedge,
retarding death.

My birthday was near yours,
in earlier sun and leafgold
of the year's decline.
You live on yet in me,
the last to hold
you here in memory,
and we'll together see
bud and flower unfold
some few times more.

Your ceased anniversary
kept in the heart
across bare fields of time
leaves a grain of what you were —
all we can say:
the rest is faith or silence —
seed at best
I'll try to nurture, sow
on my arid way,

sensing you near
in this November air,
most dear one from earth's past,
to breathe again a warmth,
light a strength.

# MENTOR

*For M.L.*


A gleam of winter sun evokes
your Italy.

                        So many years
since illness stopped you — unaware
the latest visit was the last,
your finds a memory's journey.


The roads I walk
are grey, out of June's high yellow.

But I walk.
                        I battle
mechanisms of survival
in timetable, supermarket.

But I can.
                        Sleepless,
I look at stars' ringing chorale
to this inadequacy, cold.

But stand
            and listen.

Spring rains its scent of the unmet.

But I wait to move
                in it.

I'll go again
to an Italy peopled just
by unstilled ghosts of my once dreams.

But I make
                arrangements.



Teach me your fortitude to live
an end — now unbelievable —
to what's been loved.

# TO ANNE

You'd be an old woman now,
that curling gold hair white,
your body lost in fat
or little changed, hollowed by,

if not some disease, just years'
sinew-fingered sculpture
to down-drawn lines, posture,
the bent bones. Would I know yours

among faces in the street,
would anything be left
of the amused but soft
detached intellect that lit

the shown beauty I desired,
but which, not wanting me,
was but (often barely)
patient, tolerant, while bored.

Lastingly there would have been
some wry love to wonder
if I met you somewhere
what, you present, would remain

of that young silly passion:
to know if one were still
not wholly clear of thrall
or free after long season;

if, done with your other life,
you might have turned to me,
and any more would I,
then, have borne your grant in fief?

But this, well into your own
days and a marriage, you
would also keep from me
when you died aged twenty-nine.

# IF AGAIN

Ever circling date when you had to leave me
swings again this way with the turning season,
and I know that you when you were would wonder

where I have got to.


I've an aching fancy to meet you some time,
though in states familiar can't be likely:
in the shaping they would by then not be and

how should we know us?


Much has happened through papers years without you,
much that's not much and you away unmeaning.
Yet I hope that you would accept with gladness
some things managed I now so long to tell of —

but in what language?


# OBITUARIES IN AN ALUMNUS REVIEW

It took the unprécised time
and being of a life to print
the spared line or two
of certain facts.

An extract has been pressed:
whether the wine, the spirit,
or the sludge and husks.

# SUMMER'S LEASE

The shadows stretch, day long.
Ringed and stripped of beams
the equinoctial sun
turns cautiously
on unaspiring inshore arc
across hazed blue.
Its light oblique,
it meets the eye as if
with boldness worn to mask
a face lost in power's eclipse.

Oleanders' crêpe pinks, whites,
wilt bravely on.
Fervid gold and orange blooms
simmer in the geometric beds
below palmettos and the pines.
Children are back to school,
the young and middle-aged
of May to August flown,
their struggle long resumed
elsewhere.

Warm sea and land are summer still.
By Grasse and Vallauris
grapes ripen on the slopes.
But in evenings abruptly cool
men pull on sweaters.
Coats and jackets promenade
while a tilted, puffed half moon
of cloud-smoked crimson
speeds as if caught out
at something shameful
into the velvet soot
of the nine o'clock sky.
The year is halfway down
its slide from June
to change and the North's dark.

Left to the younger old
and elderly,
pleasure now is haltingly trailed.
Days of air and beaches yet,
more room in the evening cafés,
with a sense, though, of somehow being
out of time, on truant run,
or in recovery from
some flood of malady
whose recent ebb
daren't quite be owned.
So strength with trust is breathed,
for what the year's last
may hide.

Along the coast roads at night,
voice-overing the plash of waves,
traffic, red- and yellow-eyed,
spins as ever
towards spring.


## FROM THE PINÈDE, JUAN LES PINS

Ten a.m. The sun in finest shards
of golden glass splinters through, now clears
umbrella pines. The *Golfe*, cool grey, as
the best postcards too true to be blue,
calm, a tablecloth of sheer lawn, is
patched with lighter, darker crawls of tint.
Sailing-craft, sloop- and ketch-rigged, the odd

motor yacht, and blobs of markers, buoys
are placed on it. The *Croisette* point gleams
a white bar. The sylvan *Cap d'Antibes*
looms hazy-dark behind the morning.
Of indigo wash, like a longest
barely surfaced whale of other seas
with tree stubble faint along its back,
the *Îles Lérins* stretch between the horns
of the view, where sky, a paler shade,
drops to touch the straight-ruled water line.
Heat's veil means the *Estérel* massif,
compelling jagged violet backdrop
when the mistral's blown, won't be on view
today.

                Tree shadows slope and
point among the fallen cones, clusters
of silver *boules* on powdered soil, at
cracks and shouts of middle-aged and youth-
sprinkled *pétanque*. The shadows will not
shorten much before they turn, grow long
again with the sun's swing in the year's
lowering arc.

                It's October ninth.
A pleasure powerboat, distant, rips its
finger-painted streak of foam. Cuts out.
A nosing dog, fawn-furred, spanielish,
rolls on his back. As tail, legs, head wave
back and forth in the air, he growls and
emits short barks — in ecstasy of
some relief from itch? His coat looks thick
and sound enough, if dull. Belonging
to a bathing beach with restaurant,
he attests to nourishment. No sign
of mange. Fleas then, or just an elding
and eccentric hound rejoicing like
us humans in the sun?

# BATHER

He was stepping carefully into the sea, an old man
past seventy or so, with red bathing-shorts
and a fringe of white hair, his skin wrinkled brown
by many summer suns, and slack over thin
legs and arms: pot-bellied.

The eyes were remarkable: big, dark, benign —
fulfilled. He might have been (in that place where
such people are, in summer) a person of distinction
as the world knows it — writer, painter, something
of that sort; or again, perhaps not: though this was no
matter of importance.

He advanced slowly, for the beach was pebbly there;
the waves lapping up, near mid-way up his body; his arms
swaying straight, at an angle, to steady him. And finger-
tips brushing the bath-warm sea, he moved forwards
    among

the ear-splitting pleasure squeals of children, the fewer
    adults,
the dogs' ecstasy, dotting heads on the surface, and
    flashing spray.
And some of the children pointed, and giggled at the sight
of a man so very old there among them and their fun
in the bright blue. But he was

smiling, aware of them, and yet not aware,
or not minding. Their amusement (because he was
so old, and out in the water) was not something
that disturbed, for it too was a small part
of a total joy.

Whatever it had all been about was presumably behind him;
for better or worse, it was done with, and now he was free
to be himself, as in youth: released from the taut necessity
of keeping on. And I

somehow envied him (wrongly no doubt, for one thinks
of other lives in terms of one's own: seldom
a valid frame of reference), without knowing anything
about him, except the serenity and joy I saw
on his face, at being still there, yet again,
in the summer sea.

## TIME CAPSULE

The postcard among old stuff —
a holiday near home
a view    the words    though they're
not the important thing —

out of a time    you happy
sealed in the hour's joy
from stress of days
and fears

again comes to me    now
from out of time

where    I'd believe
you're free again
                    from these

a capsule of your love

# GENTLEMAN OF THE ROAD

They called him Packman Will. His real name
and earlier story had not journeyed with him
from some long-receded past. He was a tinker —
no, not quite. A traveller of roads,
let's say, of a kind once much around.
He lived by hawking his small goods
about the countryside from back door
to back door of seeming affluence.
A coffin-like wooden box, worn shoulder-slung
by a strong, broad canvas strap, held matches,
buttons, pencils, pens, boot- and shoelaces
(leather, cotton), ink, and wool for darning,
sewing kits, little dolls, twine, writing-pads,
fly-paper, sulphur candles, mousetraps, oh,
much else. His prices were obsequious, but
he'd beg sometimes a handful of dry tea
and sugar, boiling water, milk, stale bread.
His dress a cassockish long coat, of which
the effect was dark. A blackened, sat-on hat
down-draped his head, but falls of hair fringed out
to fill like drifted snow the space between
the brim and collar at the back. He wore
the dignity, priest/doctor-humble-yet-
insistent, of a pride in service to his haunts,
appeared to thread a livelihood together,
though it was not pronounced if he'd a home,
or where he slept. Passing clean and neat,
to hippies, travellers of today, he'd seem
a businessman sold to the system, lost.
At times he'd husk his thoughts in breathy snatches
to imperious maids, brisk housewives, casual passers
friendly in the lanes. And those who cared to look
could see he had kind, sad, wondering eyes.

He was a seasonal clock, a signpost,
milestone to the ones who peopled roads,
on foot, by (still) the horse-drawn carts and traps,
or the infrequent 'twenties cars, like someone
in a Thomas Hardy novel or pen sketch,

a solitary, walking, upright stroke
which made the far-diminishing way ahead
seem longer, destiny-directed, lonelier.

Through tides of years he'd breasted air, weather,
towards an uncharted landfall, with his load
of findings offered back again, and the wisdom
he had gleaned. He'd coped with every turning,
its fresh start in different prospects, till
each most recent might have been the last,
for the road now was almost straight, homing,
it seemed, faster, to some end. But still
it was the road he travelled, and he was not
tempted off.

          Oh, he had felt things, picked up
inner warning notes that made him stop,
like a rustle behind the hedge on a dark night
in autumn, or the sudden unplaced noise
in the house where one lives alone, different
from its organic sounds, mute, as long known.
But not such as made him turn and search,
or eye the moment fixedly, and he'd started back
into the tread and movement of the self's
so long heard footsteps, not to admit this strange
invisible companion on the way,
not gone where the path might make a sudden end,
stepped off the cliff.

He did not hear then his own cry for help,
from the help that might have been out there
in the creeds and systems of belief,
or in his given, not ultimately tried,
instinctive animal resource for fronting
what was lastly urgent, menacing.

And yet he must have yielded that that time
was any time, and should be felt as now,
if he were not to be dropped, the breath knocked out,
where the road in a landslip fell away beneath him,
worth a pause, in the deceptive nerving safety

of the hold on course proven to tramp down fear,
to live it in his mind, as it would be.

No one here could say whether, as the snow
swansdowned winter trees, or from some barn
he issued, wondering at a spring dawn, he listened
to that cry.

After one summer when the June ferment
of parsleys frothed with white the verges' emerald
and July thunder drenched the empty fields,
he was not seen again.

## THE FIELD

The mouse weaves its stir
in summer grass lost
in lift of the wind's sheen.
Threads in snow score the field.
Filigree of leaf, creature's skeleton
crumble in earth,
blow as spring dust.
Crossed with moments,
furrows on sea,
the clay flows
inside hedge and bank
of a cycle's unchange.
Tomorrow they will bulldoze hedge and bank
in a rearrangement which still keeps
raindrop and stir of grass, flesh's pouring,
tracks,
changing the soul —
only, it is disturbing
to see the landscape disjoin.
The forms bodied by features seem
to contain us.

## GRASPING AT TIME

Today
birds veer.
Again it's spring
and soon
it will be summer
hurrying through.

The clouds pass, high
and slowly,
echoes in a dream,
or on the gale
a speeded film.

No time,
they seem
to cry.
Not long.

At death
what thoughts
will vie:
are such the images
that flee.